Remembering Baymore

By Peter E. Gollub

Illustrated by Marion Erard

Able Raven Press

Natick, Massachusetts

www.ableraven.com

Printed in the United States of America

ISBN-13: 978-0-9860968-0-8

DEDICATION

I dedicate this book to the children
who will wrestle with grief arising from the loss of their pet.

It is my hope that this tale will demystify or validate some of the feelings
those children may experience and help them to begin processing

those feelings, and ultimately to accept their loss.

CONTENTS

ACKNOWLEDGMENTS

To my family, for their tireless love, patience and support, and
to Ed Colozzi, for his unflagging encouragement.

1. DISCOVERY

Faye gingerly lifted Baymore's worn brown collar from the hall table and cradled it. Without making a sound, she stepped out the doorway and slowly closed the door behind her. Clouds of ragged gray wool blanketed the sun, but the swirling wind made her squint.

Faye walked. She didn't think about where she was going; she just walked. She wandered face-first into the pushy wind, toward Galdor's Rock.

Galdor's rock was a massive boulder that marked the entrance to her family's farm. Flecks and chunks of shiny mica dotted Galdor's rock from top to bottom. When the sun shined, Galdor's rock glittered like a diamond, and at night in the moonlight, parts of the mottled gray rock glinted like stars. Faye thought the rock was magical, even though no mica flecks sparkled their magic at that moment. She often climbed atop the rock when she wanted time alone, to sit and to think.

Once Faye had climbed onto the rock, she picked up a few of the small sharp pebbles on the top of the rock, and flicked them off the edge, watching them skip and plunge to the ground. She stared at Baymore's collar, and wondered exactly what it meant that Baymore had died.

A squirrel on a nearby oak branch looked at Faye and barked a chirpy warning to her, "keck-keck!" Faye turned to the squirrel and sighed, "I'm sorry Mr. Squirrel. I wish I could talk with you, I truly do. But I don't understand animal languages." The squirrel began eating the inside of an acorn as his slender branch bobbed in the wind.

Faye lifted Baymore's thick leather collar. It rested heavily in her hands. Faye felt a bit numb, holding Baymore's strong collar aloft, without a strong dog filling it. She held the collar above her head, framing the glowing clouds, as if she could collar and harness the sun struggling to shine through. The collar seemed to grow heavier. Wondering how Baymore must have felt wearing his collar, Faye lowered it delicately, as if she were crowning herself. The collar slipped over her head, and Faye let the edges rest on her shoulders. One edge of the burnished leather rested firmly against the back of her neck as the tarnished buckle slid down her chest.

Then Faye heard a high-pitched voice to her side remark, "oh, that was such a good acorn. Yes it was, yes indeed."

Faye looked left and saw nobody. She saw only the hungry squirrel, busily cleaning his front paws. Speaking softly in the squirrel's direction, Faye asked, "Did you just talk?"

"Yes, of course I did," said the squirrel, who continued to tidy himself.

Faye inhaled sharply through her wide-open mouth. She paused.

"I can understand you!" she exclaimed.

"And I understand you," the squirrel confirmed. "But I'm too busy right now to chat."

The squirrel turned and spiraled down the trunk of the massive gnarled tree that cast a faint shadow over Galdor's rock.

"Wait," Faye pleaded, "I want to talk with you." Faye stared at the vanishing squirrel without blinking. In fact, she didn't notice the black and chestnut colored owl that had landed silently on another branch overhanging Galdor's rock.

"You don't have to yell, you know. He won't answer you," said the owl, looking down upon Faye.

"Who said that?" Faye said, as she looked up.

Gliding down to the top of the rock in a loose, silent spiral, the mottled owl said, "I did. By the way, you may call me HUNTLEY."

"I understand *you*, too? What is happening to me?" Faye asked.

Remembering her manners, Faye formally introduced herself to Huntley, and explained that she lived here on her family's farm. Huntley rotated his head to peer at a distracting noise, and then turned back to blink at Faye as she scrambled down Galdor's Boulder.

"This is weird," Faye mumbled, "I don't understand why I can understand and talk with a squirrel and an owl. I wish so much that Baymore were here, so that I could talk with him too." She sighed.

"I'm still here Faye, and listening," Huntley said.

Faye looked at her legs and arms, not truly sure if they were going to look the same as they had five minutes before. She wondered if talking to animals might even cause her to grow feathers or a tail.

"Huntley, I'm confused," Faye said.

As Faye stared at the meadow grass waving in the swirling breeze, she felt her eyebrows coming together, as if they were squeezing out a thought. Huntley said, "Faye, sometimes, a strong hard wind will blow me toward a field I've never visited, or toward a meadow I didn't plan on visiting, or even blow me toward a place I want to avoid. I've learned that when the wind is very strong, sometimes I have to glide along with it until it grows weaker. Maybe you are just feeling your own wind right now, blowing inside your thoughts."

As Faye rubbed the crease between her eyebrows, Huntley continued, "If you just follow your own wind instead of fighting it, perhaps you'll find your own way to understand and accept Baymore's death." Faye chewed her lower lip silently and stared at the ground.

Huntley asked, "would you like to wander with me while I hunt? I'm usually still sleeping at this time, but I woke up hungry this afternoon."

Faye nodded. She adjusted the collar resting on her shoulders, and felt the thickness of the worn leather. She couldn't think of many things that were both so flexible and strong at the same time.

"Huntley," Faye asked solemnly, "will you be my friend?"

"I was your friend as soon as I met you, Faye."

With that, Huntley leapt into the air, and flew above the dirt path toward the rabbit hutches.

"Follow me Faye, if you can!"

Faye ran after Huntley as he flapped silently above the brown rubble road leading away from Faye's house.

Sullen stone barns stood between the oaks and elms that edged the rubble road. The lichen-splashed trees seemed to watch over the road like gnarled, swaying guards.

When the wind blew through the leaves of those ancient trees, Faye wondered if the wind's watery hiss was actually the sound of the trees whispering their secrets to each other. Faye approached the farm's lower pasture. A three-sided stone hut in the meadow occupied the closest fenced corner. During harsh weather, it sheltered a small flock of white sheep that were grazing contently in the pasture.

Huntley landed on a tree branch overhanging the pasture fence and stone hut. He said, "Anyone here you'd like to visit?"

Nodding, Faye carefully climbed over the splintery wooden fence, and walked up to one of several elevated wooden cages sheltered by the overhang of the hut's roof. A worn shovel and pitchfork rested against the cage's edge, and she moved them gingerly as she softly beckoned inside the cage's wooden hutch. Huntley watched from his tree branch.

"Helloooooo…," she called, "Springtoe?"

A large black rabbit hopped out of the hutch while several additional pairs of eyes peered from within. The rabbit glanced quickly at the owl and then hopped back in his hutch.

"Springtoe, do you know about Baymore?" Faye asked. She could see a nose and whiskers, twitching nervously just inside the hutch, but Springtoe and the rabbits remained still.

Faye continued to talk to the silent hutch. She heard only the gusts of wind puffing against the corners of the stone hut.

"Huntley," Faye said, "I don't know why Springtoe won't talk to me. I want to talk to him about Baymore's death." As she began to return over the fence, she failed to notice an approaching sheep. As Faye peered back at the hutch she noticed the ewe and exclaimed, "Lana, you scared me!"

9

"That can happen if you're concentrating hard on something," Lana said thoughtfully, chewing her cud, "but are you sure that Baymore died?"

"Huntley, what does she mean?" Faye asked.

"Faye, could you be wrong?" Lana asked, "is it possible that Baymore is still alive, and you have simply made a mistake? Perhaps you're wrong, and any minute he will come tearing around the corner of a barn to slobber all over you," Lana said.

Faye hoped that Lana's idea was right, but Faye didn't think it was – like the way she hoped a quick sparkle in a shallow stream might be a dropped coin, but usually wasn't. Faye was sure that she had heard her parents correctly.

However, Faye wondered why Baymore died, and she wondered why he had died *now*. Her feelings and her hopes didn't fit together. She felt tired suddenly, and she sat down on a patch of grass, nibbled short and smooth by Lana, who resumed grazing.

As Faye sat, two ravens became curious about the small gathering. They landed on the split rail fence beside Faye and both shouted at each other with crackling CRAWK - CRAWKs. As a light rain began to drape mist on the ravens, they both shrugged their wings as if they were pulling jacket collars tight. Huntley eyed them closely. From the fence, the smaller raven chattered at Faye.

"What did we miss?" cawed the raven, named Rawk.

Rawk leaped from the fence to the ground and hopped over to Faye like a crisp leaf might skip along the ground on a windy fall day. The larger raven, named Clack, stayed on the fence, cocking and twisting his head as he listened to Faye.

Huntley shifted his stance uncomfortably and continued watching the ravens.

"Were you crying just now?" asked Rawk.

"Maybe a little," Faye paused, "I'm not sure what to think about Baymore."

"Ahh…" Rawk said, wiping both sides of his beak on his leg.

"He died," Faye explained.

"You *think* he died," Lana interrupted, through a mouthful of clover.

"I see." Rawk and Clack looked at each other.

Clack chattered to Rawk and then he spoke to Faye.

"Young lady, death can be confusing. It's OK to cry, if that's what your body feels like it has to do."

"I still feel bad," Faye said.

"You will be less confused when your mind is ready to figure things out." Rawk said, as Clack croaked in agreement.

"When will that happen?" Faye asked softly, touching her fingertips to her lips. "I don't know the answer to that any more than I know when I'm going to find my next meal."

Clack gazed at the clouds and coughed out a rattling croak to indicate that the rain might be stopping. Rawk added, "Faye, some things take time." With that, Rawk and Clack both leapt into the air, flapping noisily as they ascended into the billowing breeze.

3. FRUSTRATION

Huntley said, "Faye, let's not stay still – let's go."

Faye followed Huntley as he glided over an uncut meadow nearing the bull's paddock. Faye plowed through the tall grass, and she liked the way the stiff strands swished against her legs as she waded through them. The grass seemed to weave together, urging Faye to slow down. But she kept moving, as if she were an unstoppable ocean wave tumbling onto the shore.

As Faye approached the fence around the bull's paddock, she stepped up onto a pile of freshly mounded earth. Her feet sank gently into the fresh soil a bit, creating two small new craters in the mound. Faye closed her eyes and inhaled slowly through her nose, savoring the damp, velvety smell of the earth. She let the earthy aroma wrap around her like a soft cool towel, but her eyes abruptly snapped forward when a steamy exhalation startled her.

Hornsby the bull squared himself to the edge of his paddock fence across from Faye, standing dreamily on the earth mound.

Hornsby snorted, "Do not come into my pasture."

Faye didn't realize that the fading musk of a hole-digging badger had tickled Hornsby's broad black nose. It wasn't Faye's fault that Hornsby shifted his contempt from the badger to her. Even with the fence between them however, Faye did not dare to move.

"I won't enter. I promise," she said meekly.

Hornsby heaved his head mightily left and right, and then he butted the nearby fence post near Huntley. The fence rail shifted, and Huntley flapped his wings to regain his balance. Faye felt the bull's movements in her feet.

Hornsby's shoulder was higher than Faye's eyes, and his ominous head seemed like it was as big as her body. He was as dark as coal, and where the peeking sunshine struck his side, his coat seemed even blacker, not lighter. The sunshine glistened off his wet nose, dark and shiny like a pond at night. And Faye could not stop staring at his long, curled eyelashes.

Huntley interrupted Faye's trance-like gaze at Hornsby, "Faye, look down."

At Faye's feet, a frowning badger drummed his sharp claws on the ground impatiently.

"Oh I'm terribly sorry," Faye said, gently stepping off the mound.

"I worked very hard on my latest tunnel, and I would not appreciate you collapsing it," said the badger as he waddled away.

Frustrated, Faye exclaimed, "I didn't mean to do anything wrong, so why am I getting criticized, *again?*"

Hornsby continued to stare at Faye, without blinking the long eyelashes she liked. Hornsby's breath steamed stiffly from his nostrils. Faye looked away, and then looked squarely at Hornsby.

"And I really don't need any more trouble from you, you big… bull-bully!"

As soon as Faye spat the words from her mouth, she froze, motionless. She tried to grit her teeth together to keep more words from spilling out, but her jaw seemed to hang open on its own. Huntley's head swiveled, looking back and forth at both Faye and the mighty, horned creature.

Faye, Hornsby and Huntley were silent. Faye's feet started to ache as she waited for what seemed like a long time. Then Hornsby spoke, as quietly as a calf.

"Faye, you are right. You've done nothing to bother me today." Hornsby paused. "Sometimes I feel ornery when I can't figure out a solution to my problems. Sometimes, my anger feels like a wild herd stampeding inside me." Hornsby paused, pawed the ground, then said, "today, I'm not angry at you, I'm angry about Baymore's death."

"I thought you didn't like Baymore."

"Not true. But I certainly did not like when he ran circles around me endlessly,

15

staying barely out of the reach of my horns."

Hornsby paused when he noticed Wilfynd, the farm's other dog, trotting in their direction. Huntley hoo-hoo'ed an alarm and flew to a high branch in a nearby tree. He observed the approaching dog from what he thought was a safer distance.

Wilfynd knew something about pleasing his human masters. He ignored Huntley and Hornsby and sat directly in front of Faye. Wilfynd immediately saw Faye's sour face, and said, "Faye, I miss him too."

"Maybe more than anyone, I'd guess," Hornsby snorted.

Wilfynd snapped at a fly near his head and continued. "Earlier, I wondered, if I had been a better dog, might he not have died? Or that maybe, if I were a really good dog for a while, perhaps Baymore could he still be here – I asked myself those questions."

"I wondered the same exact thing," Faye said. She looked straight into Wilfynd's amber eyes and asked somberly, "Wilfynd, did *I* do something wrong?"

"No Faye. Not at all," Wilfynd said, "it's not *any*body's fault." Wilfynd barked crisply to emphasize his point.

Huntley interrupted his silent, thoughtful listening to add, "angry feelings can be like the strong wind I told you about. Fighting that wind will tire you and won't solve your problem. You can change direction or wait for the wind to fade."

Faye did what felt right to her. She leaned forward, hugged Wilfynd around his long sturdy neck, and stroked the wiry gray hairs on the top of his head. She heard

his wagging tail brushing back and forth, sweeping the dirt behind him.

Wilfynd craned his head to sniff at Faye's tears, but he didn't say anything.

Hornsby slowly lumbered to the other end of his paddock.

Faye kissed the top of Wilfynd's head hard enough to make her bottom lip sting for a second. Wilfynd sat obediently.

Faye looked over her shoulder. Huntley said, "Don't worry Faye, I'm coming."

4. Convalescence

Faye walked up the pebbled incline toward a stone sty dappled with lichen and ringed with moss. Huntley flapped silently behind her, climbing and swooping in the breeze. The cloaked sun ushered aside a few milky clouds, dulling the chill from the edged wind. Faye and Huntley reached the fence rail bordering the sty. Huntley landed silently on it, immediately cocking his head to listen for mice and voles.

Inside the large sty, a lone pig lay quietly on her side. Raised spots of mud clung to her dusty, bristly hair like patches of drying plaster.

"Amelia, are you awake?"

"UNHH," she grunted. Without moving her head, Amelia opened her upside eye. The open eye rolled in Faye's direction.

"Amelia, are you OK?"

Amelia sighed.

"Can I talk with you about Baymore?"

"Maybe later, Faye. Maybe I'll feel like it later," Amelia said, lifting her head up to look more directly at Faye for a moment. Amelia scanned Faye with her upside eye, and then rested her head back down on the thick trodden bed of muddied straw.

Amelia lay still, gazing quietly at the edge of the sty. Her stare was as rigid as a beam supporting the wall of the sty.

"Amelia? … Amelia?"

"Huntley, I hope Amelia hasn't lost her hearing," Faye said.

The pig sighed, "my hearing is as good as yours, Faye." Amelia rolled onto her belly and then stood up. She grunted and wiggled her corkscrew tail to compose herself, and she began a story.

"Quite often, if my old rusted gate wasn't latched tightly, I'd nose my way out of the old pen. Baymore and I would adventure for food in the forest beginning at the edge of the pasture behind us. We would help each other look for snacks, and it was wonderful fun, every time. In fact, he was almost as good as a pig at finding my favorite mushrooms for me. That's a*lmost* as good as a pig, mind you, but not quite *as* good," Amelia said.

Faye listened carefully, as if each word was the bell-like chirp of a different songbird. "More. Tell me more."

Amelia continued, "Baymore teased me about me not being able to run as fast as he could lope, and I would tease him right back about all the briars and plant parts that got caught in his thick rough coat. When it was time to return home, he would run like a fierce November wind. Then he'd spin, roll and try like crazy to remove the burrs from of his coat before I arrived in the meadow. But that silly dog never could. We would both laugh until our sides hurt."

As she finished her story, Amelia nosed through some dirt, as if to help her remember rooting for forest mushrooms. She lay back down in the cool dirt and sighed, "Yes Faye, I miss him too. I miss him terribly." Amelia lay still again, and listened.

At that point, Faye heard the dull clanking of a cowbell. In the corner of her eye, she saw two brown shapes striding toward her. Faye immediately recognized the approaching animals as Flo the cow, and a bold billy goat named Butler.

Butler began browsing on petite white wildflowers growing at the edge of the sty.

"Hello Amelia," Butler said, "are you alright? You've been sleeping a lot, even for you." Butler continued, "instead of lying alone, why don't we do something together? I'm sure Faye would open the sty gate so that we can explore in the high meadow together."

"Not now. Maybe later," Amelia said without opening her eyes.

Faye stepped over to the gate of the sty, and jiggled the gate handle loudly. Amelia's ear twitched in the direction of the noise, but she otherwise remained motionless and quiet. Faye looked at the goat.

"Butler, what now?"

Butler chewed the flower petals remaining in his mouth as he thought about a response.

Butler said to Faye, "yesterday, I was eating some delicious plants, focusing only on the next plant and flower directly in front of me. As I grazed and grazed, I wandered myself right into a briar patch. It seemed like I was trapped, at first. It was less painful to stand still than to continue walking."

"So what did you do to get unstuck?"

"The only thing I could do," replied Butler, "I moved, one little step at a time. Until I was ready for the next one."

Huntley eyed the healing scrapes on Butler's side as Butler walked past him, looking for more browse-worthy flowers

Flo stood at the edge of Amelia's sty as Butler talked. She swished her tail and confided to Faye quietly, "I heard you talking about Baymore a moment ago. I feel bad that I wasn't always very nice to him."

"What do you mean," asked Huntley, who also listened to the entire conversation with one ear (as he listened for field mice with the other).

"Not like my cousin, Hornsby, but there were many times I kicked at Baymore."

Faye's eyebrows rose.

Flo answered Faye's look, "Baymore would run circles around me at milking time and then try to drink milk right from the bucket."

Flo belched casually and continued, "If I hadn't kicked at him as much, I wonder if maybe things would have been different."

Butler interrupted, "I disagree." He hopped up onto a barrel-sized boulder next to the sty, and turned to face Faye and the other creatures. After rubbing his chin thoughtfully on his knees, he added, "Flo, being angry at Baymore didn't cause or change anything."

Faye glanced at Amelia laying still. Butler noticed Faye looking at Amelia's motionless and blank expression. He said, "some things just take time, Faye."

Faye said, "how long?"

Butler licked his lips quickly and twisted his head upward in further thought, as if the clouds were poised to give him inspiration or even an answer. "Hmm … some things simply take as much time… as they're going to take," he replied. Faye exhaled and frowned in response to Butler's answer, and Flo rolled her big brown eyes.

"I've been hearing that a lot lately," Faye said. Huntley offered, "Faye, should we spend some time moving around?"

"Perhaps Silas and Mason would be worth talking to," Faye said, "they seem to be moving all the time."

Huntley nodded in agreement. Faye said, "Huntley, to the horse barn!"

5. Determination

Faye's quick steps crunched faintly as she jogged along the packed dirt and gravel toward the gray-planked horse barn. A narrow sunbeam poked through the clouds, spotlighting the mottled and weathered barn. As Faye entered and passed through the massive door, she thought about the immense beams overhead. Faye knew that the barn was man-made, but everything in the barn seemed primal and immovable. The thick solemn beams supported rib-like rafters that seemed unreachably high. Buttery afternoon light slid through the slender windows and seemed to follow behind her. Slanted columns of shimmering dust seemed to guide Faye toward the horses.

Faye felt small when the cavernous barn was empty, but she always felt safe there. And now, as the horses ate their evening hay and grain, the cyclic, grinding rhythm of their chewing soothed her.

Faye approached Silas and Mason, the farm's two draft horses. She had talked to them before, but she felt better now, knowing that she would be able to understand their reply. Knowing that Huntley watched and listened to her felt almost as good as a hug.

"Good afternoon, Silas and Mason," Faye said.

"And good afternoon to you, young lady Faye," said Silas, tossing his blond mane and craning his head over the door to his stall. Silas whiffed the top of Faye's head, and exhaled softly. Silas's warm moist breath smelled like cut grass.

Faye peered expectantly at Mason's muscled black neck and back, awaiting his greeting as well. Mason glanced at Faye briefly, only to quickly resume his steady munching. Silas explained, "we've both been working hard today, and Mason is very hungry."

Silas then asked, "Faye, is that Baymore's collar on your shoulders? We were talking about Baymore earlier today."

Faye nodded.

Silas continued, "Faye, we know how much you cared for him."

Faye nodded again. "I can't believe he's not coming back."

"It's hard for us to believe it, too," Silas agreed.

Mason added in his deep voice, "Silas and I know about what 'hard' is, like hard work." As Mason spoke, small clumps of partially chewed oats spattered and scattered from his mouth.

Faye said, "I wish there was a way to make the bad feelings go away or get weaker." She probed and tapped the stall doorjamb with her toe.

Silas said, "Patience and hard work will always serve as your bed and blanket."

Mason nodded and continued eating hay in agreement.

Huntley offered from his high perch, "Faye, sometimes talking with someone can strengthen your patience, no matter *WHO* you are."

Mason nodded again.

Reflecting for a moment about the way he stressed the word "WHO", Huntley stretched his wings proudly. He added, "Faye, you can always talk with me. You must know that owls are very good at listening."

As Huntley spoke, Greyleap the barn cat sprang to the top of Silas's half-door railing, Huntley abruptly side-stepped several feet along his beam-perch and bobbed his head suspiciously at the cat.

Greyleap said, "Our memory of Baymore might feel better if we focus on all of the wonderful times we had with Baymore, instead of thinking about things we can't control."

"Ughhh… that sounds like *patience,* again . . ." Faye moaned, as she let her head tilt and rock backward. Her mouth gaped open – to Greyleap it looked as if the top of her head was only loosely hinged to the back of her neck.

"It sounds like work, and I don't want to wait." Faye exhaled loudly. "I miss

Baymore *now*, and I want to feel better *now*," she said.

Silas said, "just like a bruise or scrape on the outside takes time to heal, so do hurt feelings on the inside."

Greyleap paused her grooming momentarily to add, "Faye, remembering Baymore doesn't have to *feel* like work. In fact, you might even enjoy some things that you can do to help you remember Baymore."

"What do you mean?"

Greyleap said, "consider this. There is an unruly rose bush on the other side of this barn, growing behind two hardy hawthorn trees. Baymore would always hide his favorite bones underneath that rose bush, because he knew Wilfynd wouldn't brave the nasty piercing he'd receive from the thorns of the bush and the hawthorn trees."

"Yes, I know those trees and that rose bush," said Faye.

"However, if you act slowly, and very carefully, you could dig up that rose bush, wrap it in heavy cloth, and re-plant it right in front of your house," Greyleap said. She rubbed the side of her face and whiskers against the barn stall door to mark her next thought, "seeing and enjoying the rosebush will help you to remember Baymore.

Faye's eyes flickered as she thought about Greyleap's memorial idea.

"You think I could I do that?"

Huntley interjected, "Faye, you could do most anything if you set your mind to it."

"But don't try too hard to remember Baymore," Greyleap added.

"Greyleap, what on earth does that mean?" said Faye.

"Enjoy the wonderful memories like you would enjoy the beauty and sweet velvety fragrance of those roses – gently, but with a little distance. If you cling and squeeze the roses too hard, their thorns will hurt." Pleased with his metaphor, Greyleap promptly began purring.

Faye stood still for a moment to think about what Greyleap said. The rhythm of Greyleap's purring almost lulled her into a trance.

Huntley glided from his perch and landed softly on Faye's shoulder. He was careful to balance on Faye's shoulder without using his sharp talons. Plainly he asked, "do you wish to take a first step?"

"I do." Faye replied, blinking several times. "But the problem is, I'm not sure where to start."

"Are you sure you don't *already* have some solutions," Huntley asked. "Think for a moment."

"I'll suppose I will need rich soil or fertilizer," Faye stated, nodding as she thought.
Silas lifted his massive head. He chewed noisily, stiff hay dancing from the sides of his mouth like conductor's batons. He observed, "there is plenty of manure here in the barn for fertilizer."

Faye added, "and I remember seeing a shovel next to Springtoe's hutch and a wheelbarrow by Amelia's sty!" Faye paused, and breathed deeply.

"Huntley, I think I can do this. I think I *will* do this." Faye's words sounded stronger to her than she expected, and she felt a warm pride in her neck and shoulders.

"I would even be willing to watch your work," Greyleap said, "between my naps."

Greyleap arched her back and leapt to the floor smoothly. Huntley swiveled his head warily toward Greyleap and then he returned his gaze to Faye.

"Faye, I'm terribly sorry, but it is beginning to get dark, and my hunger is returning. I must go very soon and eat." Huntley asked, "Will you be out and around the farm tomorrow?"

"Yes, I will."

Huntley said, "I think tomorrow will be a very good day."

"Will it be good because of the rose bush or something else?"

"Perhaps both. But you can't unwrap the day until it has arrived," Huntley replied.

Faye cocked her head at Huntley as she pondered his remark.

"Huntley, let's meet on Galdor's rock in the afternoon," Faye said.

Faye turned toward the dimming plank of light wedged between the towering doors. Glancing back at the animals, she tossed them a grateful wave as she strode out.

6. PROGRESS

Huntley and Faye emerged from the barn into the cooling air, greeted by a glowing horizon celebrating the day and welcoming the evening. The sun's embers had cooled to leave wispy strands of dull pink clouds draped like kerchiefs on the distant treetop silhouettes.

Faye marveled at how quickly the galloping nightfall pressed the colors of the day into the patient shadows of the fields.

The darkness slyly wrapped Faye with a chilly shawl. She began to jog, and stared at the glowing crimson band resting on the horizon. To Faye, it felt like the sky smiled its approval of her plan for the rose bush and its deep ruby blooms. As she ran, she wondered what other flowery colors she might see dancing in the embers and blue sparks of that night's fire. Faye pictured herself standing in front of the stone hearth, gazing at the split logs as they crackled, popped and sighed secrets she could not understand. She imagined the logs might convince the flame to sketch roses and leaves for her, and then erase them with each new hot flickering breath. But Faye also knew the busy heat would press firmly against her ruddy face, reminding her not to stare too closely.

Even before Faye reached the door to go inside, she felt warmer already.

THE END

ABOUT

Peter E. Gollub is a veterinarian, teacher, and attorney, living near Boston. He earned his BA in Psychology from the University of Pennsylvania, his DVM from Tufts University, and his JD from Boston University.

Marion Erard is an illustrator and animator, living in France. She studied at L'Institut Supérieur Des Arts Appliqués.

Made in the USA
Middletown, DE
04 July 2021